What
Volcanoes?

by Mari C. Schuh

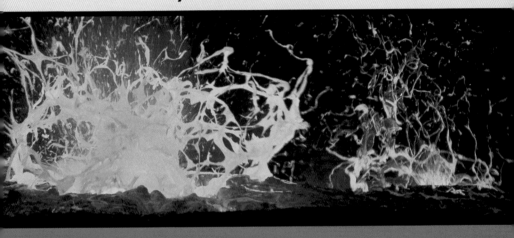

Consulting Editor: Gail Saunders-Smith, Ph.D.

Consultant: Sandra Mather, Ph.D., Professor Emerita,
Department of Geology and Astronomy,
West Chester University,
West Chester, Pennsylvania

Pebble Books

an imprint of Capstone Press
Mankato, Minnesota

Pebble Books are published by Capstone Press
151 Good Counsel Drive, P.O. Box 669, Mankato, Minnesota 56002
http://www.capstone-press.com

1 2 3 4 5 6 07 06 05 04 03 02

Library of Congress Cataloging-in-Publication Data
Schuh, Mari C., 1975–
    What are volcanoes? / by Mari C. Schuh.
    p. cm.—(Earth features)
    Includes bibliographical references and index.
    Summary: Simple text and photographs introduce volcanoes and
their features.
    ISBN 0-7368-1172-9 (hardcover)
    ISBN 0-7368-4459-7 (paperback)
    1. Volcanoes—Juvenile literature. [1. Volcanoes.] I. Title. II. Series.
QE521.3 .S38 2002
551.21—dc21   2001003763

Note to Parents and Teachers

The Earth Features series supports national science standards for units on landforms of the earth. The series also supports geography standards for using maps and other geographic representations. This book describes and illustrates volcanoes. The photographs support early readers in understanding the text. The repetition of words and phrases helps early readers learn new words. This book also introduces early readers to subject-specific vocabulary words, which are defined in the Words to Know section. Early readers may need assistance to read some words and to use the Table of Contents, Words to Know, Read More, Internet Sites, and Index/Word List sections of the book.

Table of Contents

4

A volcano is an opening in the earth. The opening is a crater or a vent.

6

Pressure builds up deep in the crust under a volcano.

8

Volcanoes erupt. Ash, gas, and melted rock called lava burst through the volcano.

Some of the hot lava flows down the sides of the volcano. Ash fills the air.

The lava cools
and hardens.

Many layers of ash and lava build up over time. They form the volcano.

Some volcanoes become dormant. They do not erupt for a long time.

Some volcanoes are active. They erupt often.

▲ Kilauea

Kilauea is in Hawaii. It is one of the most active volcanoes in the world.

Words to Know

ash—a powder that results from an explosion; ash comes out of a volcano when it erupts.

crater—a hole at the top of a volcano; a crater that is more than one mile (1.6 kilometer) wide is called a caldera.

crust—the hard, outer layer of the earth

dormant—not active; dormant volcanoes have not erupted for a very long time.

erupt—to throw things out with great pressure; when a volcano erupts, it forces out rocks, hot ashes, and lava.

lava—the hot, liquid rock that pours out of a volcano when it erupts; lava under the earth's surface is called magma.

pressure—the force acting over a given area of a surface

vent—a long, narrow passage that goes deep into the earth

Read More

Drohan, Michele Ingber. *Volcanoes.* Natural Disasters. New York: PowerKids Press, 1999.

Gentle, Victor, and Janet Perry. *Volcanoes.* Natural Disasters. Milwaukee: Gareth Stevens, 2001.

Green, Jen. *Volcanoes.* Read About. Brookfield, Conn.: Copper Beech Books, 2000.

Llewellyn, Claire. *Volcanoes.* Geography Starts. Chicago: Heinemann Library, 2000.

Internet Sites

BrainPOP: Volcanoes
http://www.brainpop.com/science/earth/volcanoes

FEMA for Kids: Volcanoes
http://www.fema.gov/kids/volcano.htm

Volcano
http://www.enchantedlearning.com/subjects/volcano

Volcano World: Kids' Door
http://volcano.und.edu/vwdocs/kids

Index/Word List

Word Count: 108
Early-Intervention Level: 15

Credits

Kia Bielke, cover designer; Jennifer Schonborn, production designer and illustrator; Kimberly Danger, Mary Englar, and Jo Miller, photo researchers

Bruce Coleman, Inc./M.P.L. Fogden, 14
David Jensen, 16
Digital Vision, cover, 1, 10 (left), 12
PhotoDisc, Inc., 10 (right)
Photri-Microstock, 18, 20
Unicorn Stock Photos/Jeff Greenberg, 4
©USGS/TASADO/TOM STACK & ASSOCIATES, 8